James W. Moore

CHRISTMAS GIFTS
That Won't Break

Youth Study Book
by Mike Poteet

Abingdon Press
Nashville

TABLE OF CONTENTS

INTRODUCTION

WHAT DO YOU WANT FOR CHRISTMAS?

Have you made a list of items that you would like to unwrap or pull out of a stocking on Christmas morning? Do you have another list of items you're planning on buying or making for family and friends?

Think back to when you were a small child. How did you approach Christmas? If you were like many children in North America, Christmas involved visiting or writing letters to Santa Claus to make sure that the jolly old elf knew exactly what you expected to find under the tree or over the fireplace. Awaiting gifts from Santa also meant watching your behavior. Santa brings gifts only to "good girls and boys." Those who are naughty can look forward to waking up on December 25 to switches and coal.

As we grow older, many of us leave behind Santa Claus traditions, but nonetheless continue to make Christmas lists and to eagerly anticipate opening presents on Christmas morning. The suggested gifts that populate our wish lists change as we age. Many young children prefer the latest and most popular toys and games but are indifferent to gifts of clothing. But as we mature, we ask for practical gifts such as clothing, as well as electronics and room decor. But while the lists we make as adolescents may look much different than those we made as children, all of these lists likely contain several ideas for gifts that won't stand the test of time.

Many children know both the joy of unwrapping a much-desired toy on December 25 and the agony of accidentally breaking this toy a few months later. Limbs fall off of dolls and action figures; game pieces go missing; other toys wear out from overuse and soon end up in attics, basements, storage sheds, and trash cans. The problem of cherished Christmas gifts falling into disrepair follows us into adolescence and adulthood. Handheld electronics are easily lost or damaged by water; clothes are easily ripped or stained; and sports equipment wears out over time.

Christmas Gifts That Won't Break focuses on different sorts of Christmas gifts, gifts that (as the title suggests) won't break or get lost or wear out: hope, love, joy, and peace. These gifts are relevant to the Advent season. We remember the hopes of those who experienced Jesus' birth and infancy, and we place our hope in Jesus' promised coming. Christ's birth was the ultimate expression of God's love for us, and God calls us to respond by extending this love to others. We see joy in the songs of Mary (Luke 1:46-55), Zechariah (Luke1:67-79), and the multitude of angels (Luke 2:13-14); and many of us look forward to joyous celebrations with family and friends during December. Isaiah 9:6, which we often read during Advent as a prophecy anticipating Jesus' birth, tells of the "Prince of Peace." Zechariah sang that, through Jesus, God would "guide our feet into the way of peace" (Luke 1:79). And, following the example of the angels, we pray for peace on earth during the Christmas season (Luke 2:14).

Hope, love, joy, and peace are gifts that should be on both our Christmas lists and our shopping lists. And they are ever-present through the greatest gift of all, the gift of Christ whose birth we celebrate on Christmas Day. Regardless of what we unwrap on Christmas morning, we should be mindful of how God's hope, love, joy, and peace are present in our lives and in the world around us. And as we do our Christmas shopping, we should strive to give gifts that express the hope, love, joy, and peace of Christ.

6

HOW TO USE THIS RESOURCE

Though this resource is intended for teens, the book itself is set up like an adult Bible study. Everyone, whether leader or participant, has the same book and literally is on the same page.

Christmas Gifts That Won't Break includes five sessions, one for each Sunday of Advent and one for each of the four Christmas gifts (hope, love, joy, and peace), and a new fifth session for Christmas Day. In this book, each session begins with a **key Scripture** and a **weekly reading**, a story about a Christmas gift craze from years past. The Scripture and weekly reading are followed by the session plan. Each session plan includes four parts.

- **Gathering in God's Light:** Each session begins with an opening liturgy that includes lighting Advent candles and a responsive reading that incorporates several key Scriptures.
- **Reflecting on God's Light:** Following the gathering, participants read and reflect on the Scripture and weekly reading. Groups can read the weekly reading during their time together, or participants can read it in advance.
- **Responding to God's Light:** Each session includes a variety of learning activities and discussion starters that explore ways in which Christians can apply each week's lesson. Groups can choose the options that are best suited to their size, setting, and learning styles.
- **Shining with God's Light:** Each session closes by asking participants to think of a gift they will give and a gift they will ask for that exemplify hope, love, joy, or peace.

The first four sessions also include seven **daily devotional readings** that encourage participants to spend time each day during Advent reading Scripture and praying and reflecting on the themes of hope, love, joy, and peace.

WEEK ONE

GOD'S GIFT OF HOPE

Matthew 1:18-21
REFLECTING ON GOD'S LIGHT

This is how the birth of Jesus Christ took place. When Mary his mother was engaged to Joseph, before they were married, she became pregnant by the Holy Spirit. Joseph her husband was a righteous man. Because he didn't want to humiliate her, he decided to call off their engagement quietly. As he was thinking about this, an angel from the Lord appeared to him in a dream and said, "Joseph son of David, don't be afraid to take Mary as your wife, because the child she carries was conceived by the Holy Spirit. She will give birth to a son, and you will call him Jesus, because he will save his people from their sins."

—Matthew 1:18-21

WHAT DO YOU WANT FOR CHRISTMAS?

If you were an American kid in the late 1970s (and particularly an American boy, though this would apply to many American girls as well), the answer to that question likely had something to do with *Star Wars*. We couldn't get enough of it! We hung *Star Wars* posters on our walls, we wore *Star Wars* T-shirts, we read along with *Star Wars* book-and-record sets. ("You'll know it's time to turn the page when you hear R2-D2 beep like this…"). And, of course, we played with *Star Wars* toys. One year I asked Santa for the Death Star play set. Nothing says "Peace on Earth" like an armored space station that can wipe out a planet with a single laser blast.

Actually, I think we wanted *Star Wars* toys because part of what made (and makes) that film so great is that it's about hope. The first *Star Wars* film wasn't subtitled "A New Hope" when it was released in 1977, but no one then missed the movie's hopeful message, or its optimistic faith in the power of good to defeat evil. On some level, we wanted *Star Wars* toys because we felt playing with them would allow us to participate in an inspiring story of hope.

The most popular *Star Wars* toys were action figures. But that first Christmas after *Star Wars* premiered caught Kenner Toys unprepared. Kenner was making mostly coloring books and jigsaw puzzles and couldn't have any plastic people from that galaxy far, far away ready by December. If it wanted to avoid dashing a lot of kids' Christmas hopes, it had to do something unexpected. So, in a move craftier than any Jedi mind trick, Kenner instead sold—an empty box! The "Early Bird Certificate Package" was a cardboard box containing a display stand (with nothing to display), a fan club membership card, and a few stickers. But it also contained a mail-in coupon guaranteeing you—if you mailed it back by the deadline—the first four Star Wars action figures as soon as they became available. Thousands of excited young fans sent in their coupons—and, sure enough, by mid-'78, these kids proudly owned 3-3/4" tall figures of Luke Skywalker, Princess Leia, R2-D2, and Chewbacca. According to the collectors' website www.starwarstoymuseum.com, "In 1978, [Kenner] sold more than 42 million *Star Wars* toys...earning an unprecedented $100 million."[1] All that success because Kenner made and kept a promise, letting young fans connect with a story of hope in an unexpected way.

Centuries before Jesus' birth, many of the Jewish people were waiting for an "action figure" of a different kind: the Messiah. *Messiah* is a Hebrew word that literally means anointed one. *Christ* is a Greek word that means the same thing. The Messiah or the Christ would be anointed, or chosen, by God to settle old scores and set things right on a cosmic scale. Many Jews remembered God's promise to King David: "I will raise up your descendant...and I will establish his royal throne forever" (2 Samuel 7:12-13). They read Daniel's vision of the future in which "one like a human being" (or "like a son of man") receives "rule, glory, and kingship" and "all peoples, nations, and languages will serve him" (Daniel 7:13-14). They read in Scripture a story about hope—the hope that God would save them, and even the whole creation, from sin, evil, and death; and they waited for one who would usher in that story's ultimate chapter.

So when Matthew says that he's going to write about the birth of Jesus Christ or Jesus the Messiah, he's raising high expectations. He is promising to tell the story of how the long centuries God's people spent waiting and hoping have finally paid off. But this will be the story of Jesus the Messiah. Contrary to some expectations, this Messiah would not be an "action figure" who brings down the evil Empire (of Rome, the political and military superpower of Jesus' day) with a flashing lightsaber.

Yet in the story of Jesus' miraculous conception, Matthew tells us that Jesus is an "action figure" in the way that matters most. Jesus' name, in fact, says it all. The name "Jesus" was common among first-century Jews. It's the Greek version of the Hebrew name "Joshua." Plenty of parents wanted their sons to share the name of the hero who fought the battle of Jericho and triumphantly led Israel's tribes into Canaan. Joshua was a "messiah" who saved God's people, but Jesus the Messiah will save God's people, not from physical foes, but spiritual ones—"forces of cosmic darkness," as the apostle Paul puts it in Ephesians 6:12. Jesus the Messiah will save people from sin. His greatest action will be his shedding of his blood "for many so that their sins may be forgiven" on the cross (Matthew 26:28).

Not everyone who was familiar with Jesus' ministry shared this belief. Some felt their waiting and hoping had been pointless. After all, what "Messiah" goes and gets executed? But Matthew is clear: In the birth of this baby, God has kept God's promises, bringing the centuries-long story of hope to fulfillment in an unexpected way. This Jesus is the "action figure" for whom Israel has been waiting.

Jesus is also the one who you and I and the world continue to wait for. We need hope today. God has given us the greatest hope imaginable in Jesus. When we trust and follow him, we participate in a story of hope that not only spans two millennia but also reaches back to before the foundation of the world "a long time ago," and stretches ahead to the very end of time. In God's story of hope, all things are ultimately gathered to Christ (Ephesians 1:9-10) and all things are finally made new (Revelation 21:5). That is our hope—and we can experience it now, this Christmas, through Jesus the Messiah, who gives freedom from sin, new beginnings today, and life everlasting.

What else could we want for Christmas, when God offers us so great a hope?

GATHERING IN GOD'S LIGHT

Leader: You will need an Advent wreath and a lighter. Select several readers to read aloud this opening liturgy.

Reader 1: At Christmastime, we hope for lots of things . . .

Reader 2: I hope someone picks up on all those gift-giving hints I've been dropping!

Reader 3: I hope we'll have snow!

Reader 4: I hope I can sleep in every day from now until the new year!

Reader 1: At Christmastime, we hope for lots of things . . .

Reader 2: I hope this year my family can get along at Christmas dinner.

Reader 3: I hope this year my family will even get together for Christmas dinner.

Reader 4: I just hope this year Christmas will really mean something.

Light one Advent candle.

Reader 1: The Lord's eyes watch all who honor him, all who wait for his faithful love (Psalm 33:18).

Reader 2: Our Lord Jesus Christ himself and God our Father loved us and through grace gave us eternal comfort and a good hope (2 Thessalonians 2:16).

Reader 3: By God's great mercy we have been given new birth into a living hope through the resurrection of Jesus Christ from the dead (see 1 Peter 1:3).

Reader 4: We wait for the blessed hope and the glorious appearance of our great God and savior Jesus Christ (Titus 2:13).

One or all pray:

Powerful God of promises,
You are able to do so much more than we can ever ask or even imagine.
May your Spirit help us find, as we celebrate the coming of your Son,
renewed hope in your presence and your love,
and renewed strength to share that hope with the world around us.
This we pray in Jesus' name.

All: God's gift of hope in Jesus Christ is the same yesterday, today, and forever! (based on Hebrews 13:8)

Share signs and words of peace with one another.

REFLECTING ON GOD'S LIGHT

Read Matthew 1:18-21. Then read "What Do You Want for Christmas?" (pages 10–12). Discuss some or all of the following questions:

 When you were a child, what was the one Christmas gift that you wanted more than any other?

What does it feel like to open a gift that you have been asking for and eagerly anticipating?

 • Many ancient Jewish people were eagerly anticipating the coming of the Messiah. How was their hope in a Messiah similar to your hope for a Christmas present?

 • When has a Christmas gift that you had been eagerly anticipating disappointed you?

 • Why might some of the people who had been eagerly awaiting the Messiah have been disappointed in Jesus?

RESPONDING TO GOD'S LIGHT

Leader: Choose one or more of the following activities and discussion starters.

Defining Our Terms

- What does the word *hope* mean?
- How do we use the word *hope* in our culture?

Look again at the Bible verses about hope quoted in the Advent candle ritual above (Psalm 33:18; 2 Thessalonians 2:16; 1 Peter 3:1; Titus 2:13; Hebrews 13:8). What, if anything, makes the Bible's idea of hope different from other ways we understand hope?

Singing of Hope

Leader: You will need your congregation's songbooks or hymnals (or some other songbooks that include Christmas carols).

Think about Christmas carols you know, and/or look through the Advent and Christmas sections of your congregation's hymnal or songbooks. Find as many references as possible to *hope*.

Discuss the following: How do these carols, hymns, and songs describe God's gift of hope in Jesus Christ? Which song contains your favorite reference to Christmas hope? Why?

Spend some time as a group singing these carols of hope. Consider planning a caroling trip to a local neighborhood or a nearby nursing or retirement home.

Symbols of Hope

Leader: You will need a markerboard, a camera, paper, markers or colored pencils, paint, and soft modeling clay.

As a group, brainstorm words and symbols that you associate with *hope*. List responses on a markerboard.

Which of these symbols, if any, do we find in Advent and Christmas decorations, songs, and traditions? (This could include church traditions or secular traditions.)

If possible, tour your church building looking for symbols of hope. Document these symbols with a camera.

Now think of all the symbols of hope you've identified, then draw, paint, or sculpt your personal symbol of hope in Jesus.

Jesus' Job Description

Not all Jews in Jesus' time shared the same beliefs about who the Messiah would be or what the Messiah would do (or whether a messiah would come). There is no easy way to summarize the diverse beliefs that people held about the Messiah. But most messianic hopes fall into three categories: hopes for a great prophet, hopes for a great priest, and hopes for a new king:

- A prophet is a spokesperson for God. While we often think of prophets as persons who foresee the future, prophets more often teach God's people how to understand God's will for the present.
- A priest is a mediator or "go-between" for God and God's people, representing each to the other. In Jesus' time, priests were responsible for performing sacrifices that made atonement for sins and put people in a right relationship with God.
- A king is the ruler of a nation or group of people.

Read the following Scriptures, which Christians often identify as promises of the Messiah. Put a "P" next to Scriptures that seem to indicate hopes for a prophet; a "PR" to those that seem to indicate hopes for a priest; and a "K" to those that seem to indicate hopes for a king. (See the Answer Key on page 20.)

___ Deuteronomy 18:15-18
___ 2 Samuel 7:12-16
___ Psalm 110
___ Isaiah 50:4-9
___ Ezekiel 34:15-16, 23-24
___ Micah 5:2-5a

Based on what you know about Jesus, how, would you say, did he fulfill messianic hopes for a prophet, a priest, and a king?

Great Expectations

The angel tells Joseph about God's great hope for the baby Jesus: "He will save his people from their sins" (Matthew 1:21). Other Scriptures about Jesus' birth, childhood, and youth also tell us about the expectations people held for the baby born in Bethlehem. Read these Scriptures and then try paraphrasing them, writing them in your own words to tell what the character(s) in each expect of Jesus.

- Matthew 2:1-6
- Luke 1:26-33
- Luke 1:46-55
- Luke 1:67-79
- Luke 2:25-38
- Luke 2:42-51

Based on what you know about Jesus, how did he meet these "great expectations"?

Option: Consider acting out these Scriptures, either as brief skits or pantomimes. Record your performances on video so that others can view them.

High Hopes

(if time)

- As you have been growing up, what hopes have you had for your life? Which of these hopes do you still have?
- As you have been growing up, what hopes have your parents, guardians, or other adults had for your life? Which of these hopes do they still have?
- What hopes do you think God has for your life? What are you doing to realize those hopes today?

SHINING WITH GOD'S LIGHT

God's gift of hope in Jesus Christ is a Christmas gift that won't break!

Divide into groups of three or four. In your groups, discuss the questions on the following page. Work together to come up with ideas to which you can commit.

- **What gift will you give this Christmas that will bring someone else God's gift of hope?** Perhaps you and your youth group could collect gifts or money for a charity such as Heifer International (www.heifer.org). Gifts of animals and agricultural

supplies given through Heifer International's "gift catalog"—
from gift packages to water buffalo!—help people in developing
countries become self-reliant, leading to a future filled
with hope.

- **What gift will you ask for this Christmas that will help you
  be a giver of hope?** Perhaps you could ask for a book of
  devotionals from a classic or contemporary Christian author. It is
  difficult to share hope with others when our individual hopes are
  low. Reading and reflecting on fellow believers' insights can keep
  us aware of God's presence and power in the world and in our
  lives, rekindling and increasing our Christian hope.

DAILY DEVOTIONAL READINGS

Commit to reading, reflecting on, and praying about one of the
following devotional readings each day during the coming week.

DAY 1: Psalm 146

Why does the psalm-singer call those who hope in God, rather than
people, "happy"? Is the psalmist talking about good feelings or something
else? Why does the psalm-singer believe that God is worthy of our hope?
How have you seen God doing these things (setting prisoners free,
opening the eyes of the blind, upholding the orphans and widows, and
so on) today?

DAY 2: Psalm 130

Hoping in God can be hard sometimes. When have you felt like
you were in "the depths"? How did you handle it? How will you express
hope in God when you are (as we all will be) in "the depths" again? Try
paraphrasing this psalm—what might a modern equivalent of "the night
watch" be?

DAY 3: Romans 4:16-25

The apostle Paul presents Abraham as a model of hope. What can we learn from Abraham's hope in God? Paul says that Abraham's faith remained strong even when he considered his body "as good as dead" (verse 19). What situations today—in your life, in your community, or around the world—seem "as good as dead"? How will you hope against hope that God will redeem and work through these circumstances? How do we know that our hope in God is not in vain?

DAY 4: Luke 1:46-55

Mary's song of praise (called the "Magnificat") is a triumphant song of hope. How does the coming birth of her baby confirm Mary's hope in God? Find and listen to a musical setting of the Magnificat. (Many recordings of the Magnificat are available through iTunes and other online music stores.) How does the music reflect the hope in Mary's words? How does being "high" or "low" in the world affect how you hear the hope of this song?

DAY 5: 1 Timothy 4:7-10

Paul tells his protégé Timothy that our hope "set on the living God" should motivate us to train "for a holy life." What do you think this training looks like today? How are you training yourself in godliness? Who is (or could be) "coaching" you as you train? What does this training have to do with hope?

DAY 6: Ephesians 1:17-23

Paul says that we only come to understand what we're hoping for in Christ gradually, as we are guided by the Spirit. How has your understanding of hope developed over your life of faith? When and where have you witnessed the "overwhelming greatness" of God's power (verse 19)?

DAY 7: John 6:60-69

Where do people in our culture look for hope? How will you, as a Christian, help others know that only Jesus Christ is the ultimate hope?

Answer Key for "Jesus' Job Description" (pages 15-16):
Deuteronomy 18:15-18, P
2 Samuel 7:12-16, K
Psalm 110, PR, K
Isaiah 50:4-9, P
Ezekiel 34:15-16, 23-24, K
Micah 5:2-5a, K.

WEEK TWO

GOD'S GIFT OF LOVE

Luke 2:15-20

REFLECTING ON GOD'S LIGHT

When the angels returned to heaven, the shepherds said to each
other, "Let's go right now to Bethlehem and see what's happened.
Let's confirm what the Lord has revealed to us." They went quickly
and found Mary and Joseph, and the baby lying in the manger.
When they saw this, they reported what they had been told about
this child. Everyone who heard it was amazed at what the shepherds
told them. Mary committed these things to memory and considered
them carefully. The shepherds returned home, glorifying and
praising God for all they had heard and seen. Everything happened
just as they had been told.

Luke 2:15-20

WHAT DO YOU WANT FOR CHRISTMAS? PART 2

For one wild Christmas in the 1980s, American kids wanted dolls. Of course, dolls were not new to kids' Christmas wish lists; dolls have been around a long time. In fact, archaeologists think the world's oldest toy might be a doll: a carved stone figure with curly hair, unearthed on the Mediterranean island of Pantelleria. Dating back some 4000 years, it's been dubbed the "Barbie of the Bronze Age."[1]

But during the 1983 holiday season, one particular doll was definitely in high demand. The Cabbage Patch Kids are, for many people, still icons of the whole decade. Introduced in 1982, these dolls were soft, chubby little figures with oddly large, puffy plastic heads, and no two were exactly alike. Children seemed to fall in love with the "Kids" at first sight, even as cynical older siblings and adults insisted the dolls were ugly. One stubborn urban legend says the dolls were created as a late Cold War-era plan to get Americans used to what we'd all look like after exposure to nuclear fallout![2]

As it turns out, the real ugliness wasn't in the dolls. A cover of *Newsweek* in December 1983 proclaimed the Cabbage Patch Kids a "craze" and "Christmas fad," but that was an understatement. According to the official Cabbage Patch Kids website, some 3,000,000 dolls had been sold by year's end, "but demand [had] not been met. The Cabbage Patch Kids Toys [went] on record as the most successful new doll introduction in the history of the toy industry."[3] The dolls proved so successful and so scarce that Christmas, some parents (and likely more than a few opportunistic collectors) seemed to stop at nothing to get them. An issue of *Time* from the same month described a few of the more dramatic—and disgraceful—shenanigans. In one West Virginia department store, 5,000 shoppers nearly rioted. In Pennsylvania, a crowd of 1,000 waited eight hours for a store to open, only to get so violent that one woman broke her leg, four other people were hurt, and the manager felt forced to defend himself with a baseball bat.[4]

At their most basic level, dolls have no function other than to be objects of kids' affection. They exist to be loved, and to help their "mommies" and (yes) "daddies" learn how to show love. So it's more than ironic that Cabbage Patch Kids inspired so much unlovable behavior. It's a pretty pointed parable of our human condition.

God created us to give and receive love. From the very beginning, when Adam fell head over heels for Eve at first sight, calling her "bone from my bones and flesh from my flesh" (Genesis 2:23), we've been made for loving relationships. So why do we, as the human race and as individuals, do so many unlovable things? God's will for our lives sounds so simple—love God and love your neighbor (see Matthew 22:37-39)—but it proves to be so hard. Each day offers us chance after chance to act in loving ways, but for each one we take, we turn down at least two more. The prophet Isaiah lamented, "We have all become like the unclean....All of us wither like a leaf; our sins, like the wind, carry us away" (Isaiah 64:6). We read the apostle Paul's beautiful words about true love—love that is patient and kind, that doesn't insist on its own way, love that never ends (see 1 Corinthians 13:4-8)—and we know that what we usually call love doesn't measure up. What's wrong with us? Why do we lose that primal, child-like, innocent instinct to love and become, in some way, one more rioting shopper, fighting everyone else off in a crazed, selfish quest for what we want?

Angels told the shepherds in the fields, "Your savior is born today in David's city. He is Christ the Lord" (Luke 2:11). And when the shepherds went to Bethlehem, what did they find? An image at once so simple and significant that it has remained one of the most commonly seen Christmas images, competition from snowmen and Santas notwithstanding: "Mary and Joseph, and the baby lying in the manger" (2:16). New parents caring for their baby—an ordinary scene, one that takes place hundreds of thousands of times around the world each day. But what had been told the shepherds about this scene, about this child, was extraordinary, and "everyone who heard it was amazed" (2:17-18). This scene of love was a sign of salvation (see 2:12). Mary and Joseph were caring for the One who cares for all; the baby in the manger embodied, as his uncle Zechariah said, "our God's deep compassion" (Luke 1:78).

The power of sin stains even our best efforts to love God and one another. But in Jesus Christ, a greater power has arrived. The letter to Titus, in verses often read in worship at Christmas, declares, "The grace of God has appeared, bringing salvation to all people.... [Jesus] gave himself for us in order to rescue us from every kind of lawless behavior, and cleanse a special people for himself who are eager to do good actions" (Titus 2:11, 14). We can be saved from the selfish stampede of sin and can learn how to really love—all because God, in Jesus, has first loved us. When we welcome him and believe in him, Jesus gives us power to become God's children (see John 1:12): reconnected with the divine love that created us, and renewed in our ability to freely receive and give that love.

What else could we want for Christmas, when God offers us so great a love?

GATHERING IN GOD'S LIGHT

Leader: *You will need an Advent wreath and a lighter. Select several readers to read aloud this opening liturgy.*

Reader 1: At Christmastime, we hear a lot about love...

Reader 2: Well, open it, open it already! I know you're gonna love it!

Reader 3: I just love hot chocolate and fresh-baked gingerbread!

Reader 4: Hey—we're standin' under the mistletoe! Must be love...

Reader 1: At Christmastime, we hear a lot about love...

Reader 2: I know we're supposed to "love our fellow man" at Christmas...but what if "my fellow man" is that guy?

Reader 3: I hate the way my family pretends to love one another at Christmas—we can hardly stand each other the rest of the year.

Reader 4: I got a lot of presents . . . but I don't feel like I got any love.

Light two Advent candles.

Reader 1: As high as heaven is above the earth, that's how large God's faithful love is for those who honor him (Psalm 103:11).

Reader 2: I am the LORD your God, the Holy One of Israel, your Savior. . . . You are precious in my eyes, and I love you (Isaiah 43:3-4).

Reader 3: This is how the love of God is revealed to us: God has sent his only Son into the world so that we can live through him (1 John 4:9).

Reader 4: I live by faith, indeed, by the faithfulness of God's Son, who loved me and gave himself for me (Galatians 2:20).

One or all pray:

Holy God,
even when we have not loved you or one another,
you have never stopped loving us.
May we celebrate, with wonder and joy,
the gift of love you gave in your Son, Jesus Christ;
and in the strength of his Spirit
may we live loving lives of service
to our neighbors and to you.
This we pray in Jesus' name.

All: God's gift of love in Jesus Christ is the same yesterday, today, and forever! (based on Hebrews 13:8)

Share signs and words of peace with one another.

REFLECTING ON GOD'S LIGHT

Read Luke 2:15-20. Then read "What Do You Want for Christmas? Part 2" (pages 22–24). Discuss some or all of the following questions.

- What Christmas toy crazes are you familiar with?
- To what lengths will people go to get popular toys and electronics that are in short supply?
- How does our obsession with getting certain items for Christmas keep us from showing God's love to one another during the Advent season?
- In what ways have you seen God's love at work so far this Advent season?

RESPONDING TO GOD'S LIGHT

Leader: Choose one or more of the following activities and discussion starters.

Defining Our Terms

- What does the word *love* mean?
- How do we use the word *love* in our culture?

Look again at the Bible verses about love quoted in the Advent candle ritual (Psalm 103:11; Isaiah 43:3-4; 1 John 4:9; Galatians 2:20). What makes the Bible's idea of love different from other ways we understand love?

New Faces at the Manger

Jesus was born to show us God's love and to save us with God's love. Too often, though, traditional images of his birth don't communicate this truth very effectively. Not only have the usual images grown too familiar—the angels, the shepherds, the animals in the stable—but also the fact that Jesus is (obviously!) an infant in the Christmas story can keep us from remembering that his mission was to grow up and give his life in love for us.

Choose one or more of the following New Testament figures, all of whom are people whose lives were changed by Jesus' love. Read their stories in Scripture. Now imagine that, somehow, these people could travel back in time to be present at Jesus' birth. How would they react? What would they do? What would they say—to the Christ Child, to his parents, even to us today?

Assume the character of one of these biblical people and create a short monologue about their thoughts and feelings at the manger.

- A man with a skin disease: Mark 1:40-45
- A small child: Mark 10:13-16
- The widow of Nain: Luke 7:11-17
- The woman at Simon's home: Luke 7:36-50
- Zacchaeus: Luke 19:1-10
- The repentant criminal: Luke 23:39-43
- A woman caught in adultery: John 8:1-11
- Lazarus and/or his sisters, Mary and Martha: John 11:17-44
- Simon Peter: John 21:15-19

Picturing Love

Leader: You will need old magazines, newspapers, and images printed from the Internet.

First Corinthians 13 is one of the best-known but least understood descriptions of love in the world. Many people know this Scripture because they have heard it read at weddings. But many people don't know that the apostle Paul was talking more about God's love for us than our love for one another. Of course, Paul wants his readers to love one another, but the love he describes is God's great love that makes all other loves possible.

Read 1 Corinthians 13 several times. Then use pictures from old magazines and newspapers, images printed from the Internet, and/or your own drawings to illustrate Paul's "love chapter." Include images that illustrate both God's love for us and ways we can love one another.

Display your work where others can see it during the Advent and Christmas seasons.

Love Feast

One way to show and share love with others is by eating together. The early church "shared food with gladness and simplicity" (Acts 2:46) as one expression of their love for God and for one another. These *agape* meals (the Greek word for self-giving love) were often connected with a celebration of the Lord's Supper (Communion). In the eighteenth century, the Moravian Church renewed this practice, calling it the "lovefeast." The lovefeast consists of simple food and beverages, provided by the community of believers—but not for themselves alone. Members invite, encourage and warmly welcome visitors to share the food and the fellowship.

Help your class or youth group plan a lovefeast during the Christmas season to which you can invite family, friends, and visitors. Include seasonal food and drink—hot apple cider and sweet rolls, for example— but keep the menu simple. Sing Christmas carols; the lovefeast is known as a musical event. Suggest conversation starters that will encourage participants to share their positive memories and experiences of Christmas with one another. For example: "What's your favorite Christmas song, and why?" "What's the best Christmas present you ever received?" "What one Christmas tradition would you absolutely not want to miss?" Above all, practice Christian hospitality by creating a warm, welcoming, nonthreatening event at which nothing is expected of your guests but their time and companionship.

SHINING WITH GOD'S LIGHT

God's gift of love in Jesus Christ is a Christmas gift that won't break!

- **What gift will you give this Christmas that will bring someone else God's gift of love?** Maybe you're thinking about giving music to some of the people on your list. Why not give them some music by Christian artists that will communicate the message of God's love in Jesus? The Christmas season offers some natural possibilities, as many mainstream "secular" artists will release holiday albums that include traditional hymns and carols of faith. But you don't have to limit yourself to Christmas music. Christian music can be found in almost every musical style imaginable, from hard rock to children's music. Provide your friend with music that proclaims the good news of God's love!

- **What gift will you ask for this Christmas that will help you be a giver of love?** Maybe you'll ask for diapers and baby blankets—no, not for yourself! You can then "regift" these and other items to UMCOR as part of their Layette Kits—essential items that mothers need to care for their newborns in parts of the world stricken by extreme poverty, natural disaster, or other crisis. See UMCOR's complete list for this and other kits, so you know what to put on your list, at http://www.umcor.org/UMCOR /Relief-Supplies.

DAILY DEVOTIONAL READINGS

Commit to reading, reflecting on, and praying about one of the following devotional readings each day during the coming week.

DAY 1: Romans 5:6-11

"Peace on earth, and mercy mild, God and sinners reconciled." What's the connection between Christmas and Easter? How do the death and resurrection of Jesus allow us to understand fully the birth of Jesus?

DAY 2: Deuteronomy 7:7-8

People sometimes act as though God spent the entire Old Testament being angry and only became loving once Jesus was born. How does the Bible itself disprove this idea? How is God's history with ancient Israel one long love story?

DAY 3: Song of Solomon 8:6-7

Through the centuries, many biblical interpreters have read the Song of Solomon as a love song between God and God's people. How is Jesus Christ "a seal" of God's love for us? What do these verses teach us about the love that he offers?

DAY 4: Hosea 11:8-9

How do these words comfort us and remind us that God will never stop loving us? How do these words call us to new ways of living? How does the birth of Jesus embody the truth that Hosea proclaimed?

DAY 5: John 1:18 (NRSV)

How does Jesus show us what it means to be close to the Father's heart? When do you feel closest to God's heart? How does Jesus keep you close to God's heart even when you don't "feel" it?

DAY 6: John 13:31-35

We don't fully receive God's gift of love in Jesus until we love others as Jesus loved us. What acts of love will you do this Christmas season that will let everyone know that you are one of Christ's disciples?

DAY 7: John 15:12-17

Jesus said the greatest love is to lay down one's life for one's friends. Jesus laid down his life for you. How often do you think of yourself as Jesus' beloved friend? How can you increasingly think of yourself this way during this Christmas season? How will thinking of others in this way shape your relationships this Christmas season?

GOD'S GIFT OF JOY

Matthew 1:22-25

REFLECTING ON GOD'S LIGHT

Now all of this took place so that what the Lord had spoken through the prophet would be fulfilled:

> Look! A virgin will become pregnant and give birth to a son,
>> And they will call him, *Emmanuel.*

(Emmanuel *means "God with us."*)

When Joseph woke up, he did just as an angel from God commanded and took Mary as his wife. But he didn't have sexual relations with her until she gave birth to a son. Joseph called him Jesus.

Matthew 1:22-25

WHAT DO YOU WANT FOR CHRISTMAS? PART 3

During the 1996 Christmas season, lots of little kids wanted a furry red monster who laughed uncontrollably when squeezed. Tyco's "Tickle Me Elmo" was arguably the decade's most memorable holiday present. It was the Nineties' version of the Cabbage Patch Kids: a toy that inspired fierce devotion among its target audience (in this case, the pre-school "Sesame Street" viewership), equally fierce loathing among cynics (the doll has been parodied in several places, including on *The Simpsons*), and ugly outbursts of violence among grownups desperate to buy it for their children. Robert Waller, a Wal-Mart clerk in Fredericton, New Brunswick, got manhandled by a crowd of some 300 late-night shoppers two weeks before Christmas. He told *People* magazine, "I was pulled under, trampled— the crotch was yanked out of my brand-new jeans...I was kicked with a white Adidas before I became unconscious." Waller suffered a pulled hamstring, injuries to his back, jaw and knee, a broken rib, and a concussion.[1]

Such scenes were a far cry from the ones that had inspired the toy's creation. Its inventor, Ron Dubren, first thought of the toy when he saw two children tickling each other and laughing themselves silly. He wanted to design a toy that could re-create what Dubren called a "feeling of utter hilarity."[2] The runaway success of "Tickle Me Elmo" doesn't just say a lot about the popularity of a particular Muppet on TV, then—it also says a lot about our desire to recapture an innocent experience of pure joy.

What is *joy*, anyway? We commonly use the word as a synonym for "happiness" or "gladness," but for Christians joy is something much more powerful. Joy was certainly powerful for C. S. Lewis, the Oxford professor and author of the famous children's fantasy series, The Chronicles of Narnia. When Lewis wrote his autobiography, he titled it *Surprised by Joy*— because real joy, for him, catches us off guard. It is not an experience we can plan; instead, joy comes unexpectedly. Lewis writes:

> Joy (in my sense) has...one characteristic, and one only, in common with [happiness and pleasure]; the fact that anyone

who has experienced it will want it again...I doubt whether anyone who has tasted it would ever, if both were in his power, exchange it for all the pleasures in the world. But then Joy is never in our power and pleasure often is.[3]

A toy might recreate "utter hilarity," but real joy never can be captured in an object. It can only be lived. Joy arrives as a gift from somewhere outside ourselves—more accurately, from someone outside ourselves. We Christians believe that this Someone is the one whom the evangelist Matthew identifies as "Emmanuel," which means "God is with us" (Matthew 1:23). Our longing for joy is really our longing for God. God answered that longing, once and for all, with the birth of a baby in Bethlehem.

The truth that God is with us is the reason the authors of Scripture can, again and again, call us to rejoice, even when circumstances look less than joyful.

So many of our culture's Christmas celebrations emphasize feeling merry. If your local radio market has, as mine has, a 24-7 holiday music station from Thanksgiving (or even earlier!) through December 25, you've likely heard more than your fair share of up-tempo summons to rock around the Christmas tree, go walking in a winter wonderland, and have a holly, jolly Christmas. Even in the best of times, the merriment can become grating. If you're facing really tough times during the holidays, it can feel like a slap in the face.

Biblical calls to rejoice, however, are nothing like our culture's incessant urging to strike up another chorus of "fa-la-la-la-la." Christians know that life can be hard. We do not deny the reality of darkness in our world and in our own lives. But because God is with us, we can joyfully profess, "The light shines in the darkness, and the darkness can never extinguish it" (John 1:5, NLT).

We tend to forget, in our Christmas Eve services of candlelight and carols, that the story of Jesus' birth takes place in great darkness. Considering first-century Jewish marriage customs, Joseph likely was in his early twenties, and Mary was almost certainly a young teenager. These two kids were far from home, having to cope with an oppressive imperial edict and an impending baby all at the same time. No one can put them up for the night, and they find no place to lay the newborn but in an animal's feeding trough. The first well-wishers are shepherds—folks not exactly considered high-class society. And, before too long, King Herod is out for the baby's blood.

That's not the Christmas story Hallmark slaps on greeting cards! That's not even the Christmas story that churches from coast to coast have their young children act out in too-big robes and cardboard crowns. It's a dark story—but in its midst and at its heart, the light of God's love shines—the light of "wonderful, *joyous* news for all people" (Luke 2:10, emphasis added). Whether we feel joyful or not at Christmas, God is with us. "Be glad in the Lord always!" wrote the apostle Paul, "Again I say, be glad!...The Lord is near" (Philippians 4:4-5).

What else could we want for Christmas, when God offers us so great a cause for joy?

GATHERING IN GOD'S LIGHT

Leader: You will need an Advent wreath and a lighter. Select several readers to read aloud this opening liturgy.

Reader 1: At Christmastime, we hear a lot of joyful sounds . . .

Reader 2: (sing) Just hear those sleigh bells jingling, ring-ting-tingling, too . . .

Reader 3: (sing) Follow me in merry measure, fa-la-la, la-la-la, la-la-la!

Reader 4: (sing) Oh, what fun it is to ride in a one horse open sleigh!

Reader 1: At Christmastime, we hear we're supposed to be joyful . . .

Reader 2: ...but I feel upset and angry because my family has no money to spend on Christmas this year.

Reader 3: ...but I feel sad and scared because this is our first Christmas since Mom died.

Reader 4: ...but I just don't feel much of anything—I mean, it's just another day on the calendar, right?

Light three Advent candles.

Reader 1: Let those who go out, crying...come home with joyful shouts...(Psalm 126:6).

Reader 2: The people walking in darkness have seen a great light. On those living in a pitch-dark land, light has dawned (Isaiah 9:2).

Reader 3: Don't be afraid! Look! I bring good news to you—wonderful, joyous news for all people. Your savior is born today in David's city. He is Christ the Lord (Luke 2:10-11).

Reader 4: Be glad in the Lord always! Again I say, be glad!...The Lord is near (Philippians 4:4-5).

One or all pray:

None other is like you, O God:
seated on high, yet looking far down
to raise the poor from the dust and the needy from the ashes.
Please prepare us:
for glad music when all is grim silence;
for bright light when all is deep darkness;
for the good news of the great joy of the birth of Emmanuel—
God With Us, now and always.
This we pray in Jesus' name.

All: God's gift of joy in Jesus Christ is the same yesterday, today, and forever! (based on Hebrews 13:8)

Share signs and words of peace with one another.

REFLECTING ON GOD'S LIGHT

Read Matthew 1:22-25. Then read "What Do You Want for Christmas? Part 3" (pages 32–34). Discuss some or all of the following questions:

- What Christmas gifts have given you the most happiness?
- What Christmas songs and traditions emphasize joy?
- What parts of the Christmas story in Scripture don't seem joyous?
- What is the difference between happiness and joy?
- How does the birth of Jesus bring us joy?

RESPONDING TO GOD'S LIGHT

Leader: Choose one or more of the following activities and discussion starters.

Defining Our Terms

- What does the word *joy* mean?
- In what ways do we use the word *joy* in our culture?

Look again at the Bible verses about joy quoted in the Advent candle ritual (Psalm 126:6; Isaiah 9:2; Luke 2:10-11; Philippians 4:4-5). What makes the Bible's concept of joy different from other ways we understand joy?

Echoes of Joy

Writer C. S. Lewis believed that we could find hints or "echoes" of joy in nature and in art.

- What in the natural world brings you joy?
- What movies, music, TV shows and books have given you a feeling like joy?
- How can these experiences be reminders for you of the source of true joy, Jesus Christ?

Breaking News of Great Joy!

An angel brought "good news" (*gospel* means good news)—"wonderful, joyous news"—to the shepherds that first Christmas (Luke 2:10). When you receive good news, how do you tell this news to others? Maybe you pick up a phone; maybe you text or tweet; maybe you update your status on a social networking site. Maybe you even send a letter (remember those?). Or maybe you just shout the glad tidings to whomever is around to hear!

Luke tells us that the shepherds told anyone and everyone their good news (2:17-18). But, for fun, imagine that those shepherds had at their disposal some of our modern technology. Working in groups of three or four, put yourself in the shepherds' position and communicate the good news of Jesus' birth using one of the following news-breaking techniques. Create a skit showing how you would spread the good news in this way, or write down on paper what you would put on a postcard or post on a social-networking site.

- A shepherd who is writing a note on a postcard for the next day's mail pickup.
- A shepherd who is texting his friends or posting updates on Twitter. (Remember text messages can include no more than 160 characters; tweets can include no more than 140.)
- A shepherd who is updating his status on Judea's most popular social networking site, Facebook.com.
- A shepherd who is being interviewed by a reporter for BNN (Bethlehem News Network).
- A shepherd who is holding a press conference.
- A shepherd with a microphone or megaphone.
- Any other creative communication technique you can think of!

After you've "broken the good news" of Jesus' birth, think (and talk) about this question: How will your youth ministry and/or congregation find equally creative ways to proclaim the gospel (good news) this Christmas season, and in the New Year?

Mary's Joys—and Ours

Leader: You will need drawing paper, colored paper, markers, beads, string, and pens or pencils.

In Europe during the Middle Ages, a popular subject for Christian devotion was "the seven joys of the Virgin Mary": seven events in Jesus' life that brought his mother joy. Although the seven events chosen sometimes varied, one commonly found list was:

- The Annunciation (the announcement of Jesus' birth—Luke 1:26-38)
- The Birth of Jesus (Luke 2:1-7)
- The Wise Men Worship Jesus (Matthew 2:1-12)
- The healing miracles of Jesus (all four Gospels)
- The Resurrection of Jesus (all four Gospels)
- The Ascension of Jesus (Acts 1:6-14)
- The Sending of the Holy Spirit at Pentecost (Acts 2:1-4)

Choose one of these traditional "seven joys" and, working individually or in small groups, create a response to it that communicates how it can bring us joy today. Illustrate it—draw a comic strip of the story, or create a mosaic using small pieces of colored construction paper. Adapt the story as a dramatic monologue or a skit. Or write a song about the story.

Try writing your own list of "seven joys"—perhaps seven people and things in your life that bring you joy; or seven moments from your past in which you sensed God was with you. Use string and beads to make a prayer rope or bracelet, with each bead (perhaps of different colors) representing one of these seven "joys" for which you can give thanks to God.

Closer Than Breath

In one of his sermons, the Rev. Dr. Martin Luther King Jr., when describing the presence of the Holy Spirit, quoted the poet Alfred Lord Tennyson: "Closer is He than breathing, and nearer than hands and feet."[4] When the apostle Paul tells us, "The Lord is near" (Philippians 4:5), that's how near the Lord is!

One form of prayer that can help us remember just how close Christ is to us—closer than our own breath—is the "breath prayer." Breath prayers are short, simple phrases, or even single words, repeated (silently) to the rhythm of your inhaling and exhaling. Spend some time now, and in the coming week, trying this breath prayer: (*as you inhale*) "Rejoice in the Lord always" (*as you exhale*) "for the Lord is near." Try adapting other Bible verses as breath prayers, too. Breath prayers can help us remember how close God is to us all the time—surely a reason to rejoice.

SHINING WITH GOD'S LIGHT

God's gift of joy in Jesus Christ is a Christmas gift that won't break!

- **What gift will you give this Christmas that will bring someone else God's gift of joy?** As angels brought good news of great joy to the shepherds, you might help others receive the good news by providing them with Bibles. The American Bible Society (https://donate.americanbible.org/) gives you and your youth ministry the opportunity to give Bibles to persecuted Christians, refugees, troops abroad, and other populations in need, as well chances to help fund the completion of translations of the Bible into new languages.
- **What gift will you ask for this Christmas that will help you be a giver of joy?** Since, as we've seen, Christian joy is rooted in knowing that Jesus is near, you might consider asking for some small, simple object that will remind you of Jesus' constant presence with you. One suggestion would be a cross or a small candle, which you could keep in a place where you'll see it often. You could, of course, use such an object that you already have; but asking for a new one as a Christmas gift might give it special emphasis as you head into a new year of developing your awareness of Christ's continuing presence.

DAILY DEVOTIONAL READINGS

DAY 1: Psalm 100

What reasons does the psalm-singer give for "making a joyful noise" to God? What reasons would you add? What does your "joyful noise" sound like?

DAY 2: Psalm 16

The psalm-singer teaches that true joy is the result of living in God's presence. How can we experience the joy of God's presence today?

DAY 3: John 15:1-11

Jesus tells his followers that "remaining" in him will make their joy complete. What do you think that "remaining" in Jesus means? How does it bring us real, complete joy?

DAY 4: 1 Peter 1:8-9

What is the connection between believing in God and experiencing joy? How difficult do you find believing in God "even though you don't see him now"? How can the promise of "your salvation" sustain you in the face of doubt?

DAY 5: Psalm 126

Remember a time when your mouth was "filled with laughter." How will the memory of that time sustain you in more difficult times?

DAY 6: Isaiah 35:8-10

Isaiah envisions the day when God will bring "everlasting joy" to God's people. Try to picture God's holy highway in your mind. What does it look like? Who is traveling on it? Where does it lead?

DAY 7: Nehemiah 8:10

How does "the joy from the Lord" give you strength each day? In honor of the ancient Israelites, enjoy some sweet food and share some of your food with those who have none.

WEEK FOUR

GOD'S GIFT OF PEACE

Luke 2:8-14

REFLECTING ON GOD'S LIGHT

Nearby shepherds were living in the fields, guarding their sheep at night. The Lord's angel stood before them, the Lord's glory shone around them, and they were terrified.

The angel said, "Don't be afraid! Look! I bring good news to you—wonderful, joyous news for all people. Your savior is born today in David's city. He is Christ the Lord. This is a sign for you: you will find a newborn baby wrapped snugly and lying in a manger." Suddenly a great assembly of the heavenly forces was with the angel praising God. They said, "Glory to God in heaven, and on earth peace among those whom he favors."

Luke 2:8-14

WHAT DO YOU WANT FOR CHRISTMAS? PART 4

During the first decade of the 2000s, lots of teens (and grownups) put games at the top of their holiday wish lists. Not just any games, though—video games.

In November 2005, Microsoft launched its hotly anticipated Xbox 360. Not to be outdone, Sony unveiled its Playstation 3 in time for the 2006 holiday season to similar excitement. Manhattan resident Angel Paredes, for example, spent three nights on a sidewalk outside a Madison Avenue store in order to be the first to buy the new gaming platform and told reporters, "It was totally worth it."[1]

The Nintendo Wii also debuted in 2006. It distinguished itself with a unique remote control dubbed the "Wiimote." The Wiimote allows players to enter and interact with various virtual environments through natural, intuitive movements. To play Wii Bowling, for instance, simply swing your "Wiimote" as you would a real bowling ball. (Just make sure it's strapped to your wrist so you don't strike the real TV set along with the virtual pins!) "Insanely popular from the get-go," wrote Tor Thorsen of www.gamespot. com in 2009, "the console was nearly impossible to find at retailers during its first year on the market. Now that it's in ample supply, the Wii routinely trounces its competitors"[2]—Although, as other companies developed Wii-like systems of their own and continue to offer newer consoles, we can expect the "console wars" to continue over many Christmas seasons to come.

What makes video game consoles so popular? Like other tech toys—from mp3 players to electronic readers—these systems appeal to us because they show off the human capacity for creation, our ability to dream and imagine. The past decade's video game systems allow us to access elaborate, fully realized other "worlds" like never before. And not just sci-fi or sword-and-sorcery worlds like those of Halo, Mass Effect, and Final Fantasy—game consoles can connect us to radically revised versions of "the real world." Remember The Sims? By 2002 this virtual simulator of such mundane goings-on as eating and drinking, making friends, and getting (and losing) a job had become the best-selling PC game of all time.[3] It was soon exported to various gaming consoles. Sports games, which have become an annual purchase for many gamers, have become increasingly detailed and lifelike, accurately and precisely depicting athletes, coaches, and stadiums. Some games simulating military conflicts also have become eerily realistic. Slate Magazine said that the game Call of Duty: Modern Warfare 2 was such an accurate portrayal of war that the violence in the game "is not easy to perform or forget."[4]

The ability to use technology to transport ourselves to other worlds and to get a taste of experiences that might otherwise be inaccessible to us is impressive and can be both educational and entertaining. But we need to think critically about the kinds of worlds that we're using our God-given imagination to dream up and immerse ourselves in. Are we creating worlds where we are free to indulge every whim, treating others as a means to getting what we want? Or are we creating worlds where we strive for what is good for everyone?

The shepherds in the Bethlehem fields may have thought they were dreaming (once the terror wore off) when they heard angels singing, "Glory to God in heaven, and on earth peace among those whom he favors" (Luke 2:14). These messengers came from outside their everyday experience—and so did the message. Shepherds weren't exactly the upper crust of first-century Mediterranean society. Respectable people didn't want shepherds hanging around. They stank, for starters—watching over dirty, smelly sheep day after day and night after night will do that to a person! And since they did have to work nights, shepherds couldn't stay home to protect their families—a hard reality that branded them with disgrace in their society. On top of all that, shepherds routinely faced accusations that they let their flocks graze on lands where they had no right to be.[5] Shepherds never found much favor in anyone's eyes. Yet they—and not the "respectable" folk—were the first to hear "wonderful, joyous news" (2:10)—the birth of the Messiah!

The angels offered the shepherds a vision of a new world: a world of justice and peace, a world where they were no longer shoved aside and where they were welcomed into the fold of "those whom [God] favors" (2:14). "To you," the angel tells them, "to you—the different, the mistrusted, the feared, the marginalized—is born the Lord!"

Don't miss this—this is radical stuff! The angels sing of a world where our usual notions of winners and losers and of who's "in" and who's "out," are shaken more vigorously than you can shake your Wiimote! The angels are signing about the same world Mary sang about earlier in Luke's Gospel: a world where God "has pulled the powerful down from their thrones and lifted up the lowly," where God "has filled the hungry with good things and sent the rich away empty-handed" (1:52-53). No wonder the shepherds hurried to that stable—they wanted to live in that world. Leaving behind their flocks (and their livelihood) must have seemed "totally worth it."

God has dreamed up a world of justice, a world at peace. And the "platform" by which we gain access to that world is "the baby lying in the manger" (2:16)—the baby who would grow up to proclaim God's special blessing upon the merciful and the peacemakers (Matthew 5:7, 9).

It's a world where God's fierce love "for all people" (Luke 2:10) means some of the people will be nudged out of their comfort, shaken out of their power and privilege. But it's a world where all the people will be at peace, for all the people will know themselves favored by God. As the prophet Isaiah foresaw, it's a world where people "won't harm or destroy anywhere on my holy mountain. The earth will surely be filled with the knowledge of the Lord, just as the water covers the sea" (Isaiah 11:9).

What else could we want for Christmas when God offers us such great peace?

GATHERING IN GOD'S LIGHT

Leader: You will need an Advent Wreath and a lighter. Select several youth to read aloud this opening liturgy.

Reader 1: Christmastime is a time for peace . . .

Reader 2: 'Twas the night before Christmas, and all through the house, not a creature was stirring, not even a mouse…

Reader 3: "I am sure that I have always thought of Christmastime… as a good time; a kind, forgiving, charitable, pleasant time; the only time I know of, in the long calendar of the year, when men and women seem by one consent to open their shut-up hearts freely." (from Charles Dickens' A *Christmas Carol*)

Reader 4: "I heard the bells on Christmas Day their old, familiar carols play, and wild and sweet the words repeat of peace on earth, goodwill to men!" (Henry Wadsworth Longfellow)

Reader 1: Christmastime is a time for peace…

Reader 2: …but our world is not at peace. Wars rage on around the globe, and acts of terror are a threat to every nation.

Reader 3: Our society is not at peace. Those most in need of charity and kindness too often go without, and justice is still denied to the poor and the powerless.

Reader 4: Our homes are not at peace. They are stirring with pain and mistrust, or resentment and anger, or violence and abuse.

Light four Advent candles.

Reader 1: A child is born to us, a son is given to us, and authority will be on his shoulders. He will be named Wonderful Counselor, Mighty God, Eternal Father, Prince of Peace (Isaiah 9:6).

Reader 2: He delivers the needy who cry out, the poor, and those who have no helper. He has compassion on the weak…and saves the lives of those who are in need. He redeems their lives from oppression and violence; their blood is precious in his sight (Psalm 72:12-14).

Reader 3: Don't be anxious about anything; rather, bring up all of your requests to God in your prayers and petitions, along with giving thanks. Then the peace of God that exceeds all understanding will keep your hearts and minds safe in Christ Jesus (Philippians 4:6-7).

Reader 4: Peace I leave with you. My peace I give you. I give to you not as the world gives. Don't be troubled or afraid (John 14:27).

One or all pray:

Most High, you rule over all,
and you command the nations to be still and know that you
    alone are God.
Speak your powerful word of peace today,
that we and the world may truly know
the freedom from chilling fear and freedom for loving service
that is found by entrusting ourselves to your Son.
 This we pray in Jesus' name.

All: God's gift of peace in Jesus Christ is the same yesterday, today, and forever! (based on Hebrews 13:8)

Share signs and words of peace with one another.

REFLECTING ON GOD'S LIGHT

Read Luke 2:8-14. Then read "What Do You Want for Christmas? Part 4" (pages 42–44). Discuss some or all of the following questions.

- In what ways are you at peace during the Advent and Christmas seasons?

46

- What parts of the Advent and Christmas seasons aren't very peaceful?
- The shepherds who first heard the good news of Jesus' birth were outcasts and misfits in their society. Who are some of the people who are ignored or left out in our society?
- How can we bring the peace of Christ to these people?

Who would be the first to hear the good news today?

RESPONDING TO GOD'S LIGHT

Leader: Choose one or more of the following activities and discussion starters.

Defining Our Terms

- What does the word *peace* mean?
- How do we use the word *peace* in our culture?

Look again at the Bible verses about ~~love~~ *peace* quoted in the Advent candle ritual (Isaiah 9:6; Psalm 72:12-14; Philippians 4:6-7; John 14:27). What makes the Bible's idea of peace different from other ways we understand peace?

Peace Puzzles

The Hebrew word for peace, *shalom*, literally means "health," "completeness," and "wholeness." In the New Testament, the Greek word for peace takes on some of this meaning as well. In groups of three or four, read and discuss some or all of the following Scriptures. How does each one describe or depict shalom? What divisions have been overcome? What do these Scriptures say about health and wholeness? Which of these Scriptures describe promises from God, which give us instructions to follow, and which do both?

- Leviticus 26:3-6
- Psalm 85
- Proverbs 10:10

47

- Proverbs 16:7
- Isaiah 54:9-10
- 2 Corinthians 13:11-13
- Ephesians 2:13-18

Then, with your group, choose one of the verses to write and/or illustrate on a piece of cardstock. Cut up your card as a jigsaw puzzle. Exchange puzzles with another group and put each other's puzzles together. This activity is a reminder that *shalom* means taking something that is broken and making it whole.

Peace and the Poor

The prophets of the Bible teach that we cannot know peace in the world without justice. We must follow Jesus' example by reaching out to those who are poor, sick, hungry, oppressed, and ignored. Read the following Scriptures. Each one looks at God's response to injustice. Beside each, describe where you see a similar problem of injustice in the world today.

- Psalm 34:11-18
- Isaiah 59:1-8
- Jeremiah 6:13-16
- Zechariah 8:14-17

Individually or as a group, contact one of your local elected officials or federal representatives about a specific issue of injustice that you identify. Inquire about his or her record on the issue and urge him or her to keep in mind persons in need when voting on legislation and policy.

Pray for the Peace of . . .

Leader: Beforehand, browse news sources to identify places of unrest around the world. Also bring sticky notes or thumbtacks, along with a globe or world map if there is not already one in your meeting space.

Psalm 122 calls on us to "Pray that Jerusalem has peace" (verse 6). The city of Jerusalem's name derives from the word *shalom*, but, even today, peace has proved elusive there. Take time to reflect on other places in the world that need our prayers for peace. Mark these places on a map or globe with sticky notes or thumbtacks. Make a list of these cities and countries and appoint one person to send this list to the rest of the group by e-mail or text message or through a social networking site. Use this list as a reminder to pray for these parts of the world.

"Peace! Be Still!" Dramatize it

Read Mark 4:35-41. In the ancient world, natural storms were, understandably, powerful symbols of all the forms of chaos that threaten us. Jesus, however, is able to bring order and peace all chaos.

As a group, read and reflect on this story using the practice of *lectio divina* ("divine" or "spiritual reading"). There is no "one right way" to do *lectio divina*; but here is one suggested method:

1. *Read the Scripture aloud a first time.* After a brief silence, identify the word, phrase, or image from the text that most attracts your attention. Spend some time meditating on that word, phrase or image.

2. *Read the text aloud a second time.* After a brief silence, try to answer (silently) this question: Where do you see yourself in this story? What message, do you think, does Jesus want to give you through this Scripture?

3. *Read the text aloud a third time.* After a brief silence, try to answer (silently) this question: Based on your reading of and reflection on this Scripture, what is Jesus calling you to do or to be this day?

4. *Close with a prayer of thanksgiving for your encounter with God's Word.*

Work as a group to do a dramatization of this story. If possible, videotape your performance and make it available for the rest of the congregation to view.

Blessed Are the Peacemakers

Jesus said, "Happy are people who make peace, because they will be called God's children" (Matthew 5:9).

- What does it mean to be a peacemaker?
- Based on what you know about peace from the Scriptures you've read and from the activities above, how would someone go about making peace?

As a group, identify someone in your congregation or community who acts as a peacemaker. This could be a person who brings hope to a neighborhood torn apart by violence; it could be a teacher or principal who is especially skilled at helping students work through conflicts; it could be someone who works vigorously to fight hunger or poverty; it could be a person who demonstrates extraordinary grace and forgiveness. If you have trouble identifying someone, scan local news sources on the Internet.

Once you have chosen your local peacemaker, determine a way that you can honor this person. This could involve creating a card or certificate, lifting up this person on your church website or blog, finding ways to tell other people in your congregation or community about this person's contributions, or making a donation in this person's honor to a cause that is important to him or her.

SHINING WITH GOD'S LIGHT

God's gift of peace in Jesus Christ is a Christmas gift that won't break!

- **What gift will you give this Christmas that will bring someone else God's gift of peace?** You could choose to support a charity that helps innocent victims of war. The HALO Trust, for example, is a charity devoted to "one of the most inherently dangerous jobs on earth," removing still-live landmines and other "debris of war" so that such devices no longer claim victims (https://www.halotrust.org/).

- **What gift will you ask for this Christmas that will help you be a giver of peace?** Consider taking a cue from Ephesians 6:15: Put shoes on your feet so that you are ready to spread the good news of peace." If footwear is on your Christmas wish list, why not ask for recycled shoes? They're out there—just check the Internet for options—and their purchase reduces your ecological footprint (literally!) and promotes the shalom of the environment. You might also ask for TOMS shoes. When someone purchases a pair of TOMS shoes, the company donates a pair to a child in need.

DAILY DEVOTIONAL READINGS

DAY 1: John 14:27

How is the peace that Jesus promises different from the peace the world can give? In what ways do we receive and share Jesus' peace?

DAY 2: Psalm 122

Spend time today in prayer not only for Jerusalem but also for all places in the world that do not now know peace.

DAY 3: Isaiah 9:6-7

Christians have long read these verses as a prophecy about Jesus. Find and listen to a recording of "For Unto Us a Child is Born" from Handel's Messiah. As you do, reflect on what it means to worship Jesus as the "Prince of Peace."

DAY 4: Mark 9:50

Why, do you think, does Jesus compare "keeping peace with each other" to salt? Make and share a salty snack with someone as an edible sign of your commitment to living in peace.

DAY 5: Luke 19:41-42

What would cause Jesus to weep over your city? How can you help show your community "the things that lead to peace"?

DAY 6: Numbers 6:24-26

Try memorizing this benediction. Remember a time when you have felt God's face shining upon you. How will your face reflect the peace of God for someone else today?

DAY 7: Colossians 1:19-20

These verses remind us why Jesus' birth is worth celebrating: He was born to die, to make peace between God and all things "through the blood of his cross." Design a Christmas card that visually shares this truth.

GOD'S GIFT OF CHRIST

Matthew 2:1-12
REFLECTING ON GOD'S LIGHT

After Jesus was born in Bethlehem in the territory of Judea during the rule of King Herod, magi came from the east to Jerusalem. They asked, "Where is the newborn king of the Jews? We've seen his star in the east, and we've come to honor him."

When King Herod heard this, he was troubled, and everyone in Jerusalem was troubled with him. He gathered all the chief priests and the legal experts and asked them where the Christ was to be born. They said, "In Bethlehem of Judea, for this is what the prophet wrote:

You, Bethlehem, land of Judah,
    by no means are you least among the rulers of Judah,
        because from you will come one who governs,
        who will shepherd my people Israel."

Then Herod secretly called for the magi and found out from them the time when the star had first appeared. He sent them to Bethlehem, saying, "Go and search carefully for the child. When you've found him, report to me so that I too may go and honor him." When they heard the king, they went; and look, the star they had seen in the east went ahead of them until it stood over the place where the child was. When they saw the star, they were filled with joy. They entered the house and saw the child with Mary his mother. Falling to their knees, they honored him. Then they opened their treasure chests and presented him with gifts of gold, frankincense, and myrrh. Because they were warned in a dream not to return to Herod, they went back to their own country by another route.

Matthew 2:1-12

WHAT DO YOU WANT FOR CHRISTMAS? PART 5

This Advent, we've looked back at some of the hottest Christmas gifts of each decade. But why does every decade—every year, for that matter—have presents like that in the first place?

In 2016, "Hatchimals" were the holiday season's most in-demand presents. They're fuzzy, battery-powered, electronic creatures that peck their way out of plastic eggs and "grow up" as kids interact with them. According to *The New York Times*, "Desperate parents intent on buying a Hatchimal [were] waiting in long lines at retailers, putting their names on waiting lists, and even buying lottery tickets for the toy. Sellers on Amazon and eBay were asking more than three times the retail price"—which was $60 to begin with![1]

I can appreciate how Hatchimals combine cute, cuddly newborn animals' timeless appeal with the electronic innovation's coolness factor. But will they still be "gotta have it" gifts next Christmas? It seems unlikely. Our society is a lot like ancient Athens, as described in the Acts of the Apostles: All the people "spend their time doing nothing but talking about or listening to the newest thing" (Acts 17:21). In other words, knowing whether a single toy or game will become the must-have item of the year is impossible to predict. We just know it will be something new. The rest is a mystery. As one toy company executive told *The New York Times*: "Nobody knows why these things happen. They're an act of God."[2]

Now, that toy exec wasn't really trying to think or talk theologically. But I find his choice of words striking. Must-have Christmas presents are "an act of God." It has me wondering: are we trying to turn Christmas presents into something they can never be? And what would it mean for us to focus on the true act of God at Christmas, which took place in the birth of God's Son in Bethlehem?

When I was a kid, adults told me the Christmas gift-giving tradition was meant to remind us of the magi, who brought "gifts of gold, frankincense, and myrrh" to the young Jesus (Matthew 2:11). Now, *maybe* you think about the magi as you're ripping the wrappings off of Christmas gifts. But honestly? I didn't then; I don't now. Our society's annual exchange of stuff, like so much about the way most Americans (myself included) celebrate the season, doesn't seem all that connected to the first Christmas. Yes, the magi gave gifts. And, sure, those gifts were hard to get—at least for poor families like Jesus' family. (Some scholars say that, among wealthy folk in the ancient world, gold, frankincense, and myrrh were actually common baby presents.[3]) But these gifts are pretty far from our minds when we're opening our own presents on Christmas.

So instead of forcing a religious meaning onto the tradition of Christmas gift exchanges, let's remember the real exchange, the actual "act of God," at the heart of Christmas: the Incarnation, the birth of God's own Son, the exchange of human power for God's power.

For all his murderous scheming, King Herod glimpsed what's at stake in the real Christmas exchange. As Herod's scribes discovered in prophecies, God was giving Israel a true ruler, one who would shepherd God's people toward greater faithfulness—not another puppet king like Herod himself, who only had power over Roman-controlled Judea because Caesar let him have it.

With the birth of the King of the Jews, God was giving the chosen people—and, through them, the world (Genesis 12:3)—an embodiment of God's kingdom. God's values and priorities, God's commitments to justice and mercy and holiness, are this new, true monarch's sole focus. Any competing priorities and claims for loyalty will have to be "exchanged"— abandoned, tossed out, left behind. But Herod's already doubled down on lesser values and unworthy commitments. No wonder he trembled at the news of the long-promised king's birth, "and everyone in Jerusalem" with him (Matthew 2:3). The birth of Jesus could not be more unlike the "birth" of a Hatchimal! Oh, I imagine he was a cute and cuddly newborn (although, if Isaiah 53:2 foresees his coming, maybe not)—but Jesus' birth demands decision and sparks division.

At Christmas, we sing carols about Jesus sleeping in heavenly peace. But grown-up Jesus announced, "Don't think that I've come to bring peace to the earth. I haven't come to bring peace but a sword" (Matthew 10:34)—the sword of God's judgment, cutting away all that doesn't meet God's standards of holiness, justice, mercy, and humble living (Micah 6:8). And grown-up Jesus told Pontius Pilate (in the only comment Jesus made about his own birthday), "I was born and came into the world for this reason: to testify to the truth. Whoever accepts the truth listens to my voice" (John 18:37)—meaning everyone who doesn't, won't . . . including Pilate, who orders Jesus' execution.

This is the great exchange at the heart of Christmas. In Jesus' birth, God calls the world to exchange ways that lead to death, both physical and spiritual, for ways that lead to life. God calls us to exchange greed, oppression, violence, and judgment for justice, mercy, and humility. God calls us to exchange selfishness for holiness. God calls us to exchange falsehood for the truth. King Herod realized this reality—and rejected it. He'd sooner kill all of Bethlehem's toddlers than submit himself to God's exchange of worldly values and priorities for heavenly ones (Matthew 2:16).

Jesus' birth calls us to exchange our old lives for new life because he exchanged his divine existence for our human one. As the Apostle

Paul writes, Jesus, though eternally equal with God, "emptied himself by taking the form of a slave and by becoming like human beings...He humbled himself by becoming obedient to the point of death, even death on a cross" (Philippians 2:6-8). God's Son, in obedience to his Father's love for sinful humans and a fallen world, "became flesh and made his home among us" (John 1:14)—the amazing mystery we Christians call the Incarnation.

Jesus traveled a different road than he might have: the road of suffering, self-sacrifice, and costly love. And he promises that those he has chosen to belong to him, those who listen to and trust his voice, will travel the road back to God with him (see Romans 6:5).

I think the main point of the magi's story isn't about giving gifts, but about committing ourselves to living life differently as a result of meeting Jesus. Yes, Matthew is, on one level, simply stating a plot point when he writes that the magi "went back to their own country by another route" (Matthew 2:12). But at a deeper level, those words describe what God wants for all of us after we see and worship the Christ Child: to spend the rest of our lives traveling to our true home country, God's realm, by a different road—a way of life that lines up with Jesus' own, a life devoted to love and service of God and neighbor.

If we want to remember the magi this Christmas, let's not do it by giving whatever "gotta have it" gift tops this season's holiday shopping list. Let's do it by doing what they did: seeing the signs of God's presence, offering Christ our worship, and then setting out for home—our real home, with God—by a different road. We cannot find or travel that road on our own, but because of Jesus Christ, God's greatest gift who is himself "the way" (John 14:6), we can.

What else could we possibly want for Christmas, when God offers us the gift of Christ?

GATHERING IN GOD'S LIGHT

Leader: You will need an Advent Wreath and a lighter. Select several readers to read aloud this opening liturgy.

Reader 1: At Christmastime, we look for a lot of gifts...

Reader 2: I'm looking for the latest video game under my tree.

Reader 3: I'm looking for tickets to the big concert this summer.

Reader 4: I'm looking for clothes that'll make everyone notice me.

Reader 1: At Christmastime, we look for a lot of gifts...

Reader 2: I'm looking for something that fills my days with meaning.

Reader 3: I'm looking for an experience that makes me feel alive.

Reader 4: I'm looking for someone to tell and show me that I matter.

Light all four Advent candles and the Christ candle.

Reader 1: In the beginning was the Word, and the Word was with God, and the Word was God.

Reader 2: Everything came into being through him, and without him nothing came into being.

Reader 3: What came into being through him was life, and the life was the light for all people.

Reader 4: The light shines in darkness, and the darkness does not extinguish it.

All Readers: And the Word became flesh, and made his home among us, and we have seen his glory, full of grace and truth. (based on John 1:1-5, 14)

One or all pray:

Loving and generous God,
You have given us the breath of life, and have promised the gift of new and everlasting life in your Son, the baby born in Bethlehem—Emmanuel: God with us!

May your Spirit help us see signs of his presence with us and with our world, and strengthen us to follow where he leads, until we at last share his heavenly home.

This we pray in Jesus' name. Amen.

All: God's greatest gift is Jesus Christ—the same yesterday, today, and forever! (based on Hebrews 13:8)

Share signs and words of peace with one another.

REFLECTING ON GOD'S LIGHT

Read Matthew 2:1-12. Then read "What Do You Want for Christmas? Part 5" (pages 54–57). Discuss some or all of the following questions:

- When you were a child, what reason(s) did you think were behind the tradition of giving gifts at Christmas?
- Why does the visit from the magi ("wise men") frighten King Herod?
- Why did the ancient prophecy (from Micah 5:2) call the promised ruler a "shepherd"? What words for or images of a ruler or leader might carry similar meanings today?
- The magi saw and followed a star. What signs of God's presence and activity in the world do you see and follow? How?
- The magi went home "by another route." How is your life different—how are you different—because you have seen and worshiped Jesus Christ?

RESPONDING TO GOD'S LIGHT

Leader: Choose one or more of the following activities and discussion starters.

Ponder the Magi's Gifts

People have wondered about and debated the meaning of the magi's gifts for two millennia. Read the Scriptures below. How might each one help us understand the significance of what the magi gave Jesus? How might each of the magi's gifts point to Jesus' identity as prophet, priest, and king, discussed in the first chapter of this book?

- Isaiah 60:1-6
- Psalm 72:8-15
- Exodus 30:34-35
- Mark 15:22-24; John 19:38-40

Pray Using an Image

Use an Internet search engine to browse images depicting the magi's visit to the Christ Child (often called "the adoration of the magi"). When an image particularly grabs your attention, pause and spend several minutes looking at it. Ask such questions as:

- What's the most noticeable feature in this artist's version of the scene?
- What interesting or important details escaped your notice at first?
- How would you describe the emotions on the figures' faces?
- How does this artist use light and darkness in the scene?
- What thoughts and feelings does this image evoke in you?
- Try imagining yourself as a participant in the scene. What do you say or do?

After a few minutes, pray a prayer that uses one or more of these answers, or some other reaction to the image, as a starting point.

Make a "Matthew 2:12 Ornament"

Leader: You will need a smooth Christmas ball ornament for each participant, several old road maps, Mod Podge or other clear sealer, and a brush for each participant.

Craft this visual reminder for your Christmas tree of the magi's return trip home "by another route," and of your commitment to travel "home" to God through life by a different "road" because of your encounter with the Christ Child.

You will need a smooth Christmas ball ornament you don't mind covering over, an old road map, Mod Podge or other clear sealer, and a brush.

Cut the old map into circles about two inches in diameter. Coat your ornament with the sealer. While the ornament's surface is still sticky, apply the cut-up map circles as neatly as possible all around it. Coat the map-covered ornament with the sealer. Smooth out any wrinkles by hand (then wash your hands). Let the ornament dry for at least one hour.

As you wait for your ornament to dry, talk with someone else about how you are "traveling a different road" in life as a result of worshiping Jesus.

(*Adapted from "Easy Decoupage Christmas Ornament,"*
www.gymcraftlaundry.com, December 4 2015; http://gymcraftlaundry
.com/easy-decoupage-santas-sleigh-map-ornament/).

Small and Simple King Cakes

Leader: You will need one or more cans of ready-to-bake cinnamon roll dough with icing, several colored sugars, one or more cookie sheets, and access to an oven.

Although, like Christmas gift-giving, the popular Mardis Gras tradition of "king cakes" has little to do with the biblical story of the magi, it is sometimes connected to the magi (three kings) who visited Jesus because authentic king cakes have miniature plastic babies baked inside. You can bake and enjoy this simplified version of the treat—and if you share them with other people, you'll be demonstrating one of the values of God's kingdom at the same time!

Separate the cinnamon roll dough into the individual, perforated rolls, and unroll each roll until you have a "rope." Twist each rope as you shape it into a circle. Bake the dough circles on the cookie sheet for 20-25 minutes at 350°F, or until golden brown. While the finished rolls are still warm, ice them and sprinkle them with the colored sugars. (We don't recommend adding miniature plastic babies to your "king cakes"—simply thinking about Jesus as you eat the cakes involves a lot smaller risk of choking!)

*(Adapted from "Mini King Cakes," https://www.pillsbury.com/recipes
/mini-king-cakes/ee5e7772-e399-49d7-b721-c46abe1fc7d5)*

Mark Your Doors with Chalk

Another old custom associated with the magi is "chalking the doors"—an enacted prayer for God's blessing on all of our going out and coming in during a new year (see Psalm 121:8). Using chalk, simply write the old year and the new on the doorway, separated by the letters "C M B," which stand for the names tradition has given the magi: Caspar, Melchior, and Balthasar. You may want to use symbols of faith like the cross or the Alpha and Omega in addition to or instead of these letters. The act is not a magic ritual, but a visible reminder of our conviction that, when we journey a different road as a result of worshiping Jesus, he journeys with, behind, and before us.

You can find a worship service to accompany this ritual at "An Epiphany Blessing of Homes and Chalking the Door," Discipleship Ministries of the United Methodist Church (https://www.umcdiscipleship.org/resources /an-epiphany-blessing-of-homes-and-chalking-the-door).

NOTES

Chapter 1

1. "Guide to Star Wars Toy Collecting (Origins)," accessed June 5, 2017, http://www
    .starwarstoymuseum.com/star_wars_toys.html.

Chapter 2

1. Jan Payne, *The World's Best Book: A Celebration—40 Years of Life* (Philadelphia: Running
    Press Book Publishers, 2009), 147.
2. Barbara Mikkelson, "Cabbage Patch Dolls: Were Cabbage Patch dolls designed to
    resemble what people will look like after a nuclear attack?" www.snopes.com,
    published May 20, 2011, accessed June 8, 2017; http://www.snopes.com/business
    /origins/cabbage.asp.
3. "Our History," Cabbage Patch Kids Babyland General Hospital, accessed June 8,
    2017, http://www.babylandgeneral.com/about/our-history/.
4. Otto Friedrich and Robert Carney, "The Strange Cabbage Patch Craze," *Time*,
    published December 12,1983, accessed June 8, 2017; http://www.time.com/time
    /magazine/article/0,9171,921419-1,00.html.

Chapter 3

1. "Just Tickled," People 47:1, published January 13, 1997, accessed June 9, 2017,
    http://www.people.com/people/archive/article/0,,20143226,00.html.
2. Louise A. Gikow, *Sesame Street: A Celebration—40 Years of Life on the Street* (New York:
    Black Dog & Leventhal, 2009), 274.

3. As cited in Wayne Martindale & Jerry Root, eds., *The Quotable Lewis* (Carol Stream, IL: Tyndale House, 1990), 357.
4. "Index of Sermon Topics," Martin Luther King Jr. Papers Project at The Martin Luther King Jr. Research and Education Institute–Stanford University, accessed June 12, 2017, http://mlk-kpp01.stanford.edu/primarydocuments/Vol6/20Feb-4May1951IndexofSermonTopics.pdf; see footnote 33.

Chapter 4

1. Matt Richtel, "Release of PlayStation 3 Becomes a Waiting Game," *New York Times*, published November 17, 2006, accessed June 13, 2017, http://www.nytimes.com/2006/11/17/technology/17game.html?scp=118&sq=Sony+%22Playstation+3%22&st=nyt.
2. Tor Thorsen, "GDC 2009: New DS Zelda announced, Wii ships 50 million," accessed June 13, 2017, http://www.gamespot.com/articles/gdc-2009-new-ds-zelda-announced-wii-ships-50-million/1100-6206693/.
3. "Best Selling PC Games," Listal, published January 21, 2008, accessed June 14, 2017, http://www.listal.com/list/bestselling-pc-games.
4. Chris Suellentrop, "This War Is Hell–Call of Duty" Modern Warfare 2 made me feel terrible about myself, and I loved it," *Slate*, published Novemeber 16, 2009, accessed June 14, 2017, http://www.slate.com/id/2235774/.
5. See Bruce J. Malina and Richard L. Rohrbaugh, *Social-Science Commentary on the Synoptic Gospels* (Minneapolis: Fortress Press, 1992), 296.

Chapter 5

1. Rachel Rabkin Peachman, "The Hunt for Hatchimals, the Elusive Toy of the Holiday Season," *New York Times*, published December 5, 2016, accessed June 16, 2017, http://www.nytimes.com/2016/12/05/well/family/the-hunt-for-hatchimals-the-elusive-toy-of-the-holiday-season.html.
2. Ibid.
3. Richard R. Losch, *All the People in the Bible: An A-Z Guide to the Saints, Scoundrels, and Other Characters in Scripture* (Grand Rapids, MI: Eerdmans, 2008), 269.

CPSIA information can be obtained
at www.ICGtesting.com
Printed in the USA
LVHW01s0507090817
544291LV00004BA/12/P